BARKCUTERIE

BARKCUTERIE

Over 25 Pawsome Snack
Boards Your Dog Will Love

HAMMY & OLiViA

ROCK
POINT

First published in 2023 by Rock Point,
an imprint of The Quarto Group,
142 West 36th Street, 4th Floor,
New York, NY 10018, USA
T (212) 779-4972 F (212) 779-6058
www.Quarto.com

Printed in United States of America

Rock Point titles are also available at discount
for retail, wholesale, promotional and bulk
purchase. For details, contact the Special Sales
Manager by email at specialsales@quarto.com
or by mail at The Quarto Group, Attn: Special
Sales Manager, 100 Cummings Center Suite,
265D, Beverly, MA 01915, USA.

10 9 8 7 6 5 4

ISBN: 978-1-63106-928-4

Library of Congress Control Number:
2022944904

Publisher: Rage Kindelsperger
Creative Director: Laura Drew
Editorial Director: Erin Canning
Managing Editor: Cara Donaldson
Editorial Assistant: Katelynn Abraham
Hammy and Olivia Photography: Rick Vierkandt
(except page 86 image by Chris Equale)
Food Photography and Styling: Laura Klynstra
Cover and Interior Design: Laura Klynstra

Remember, the health and safety of your pets is top priority, as you know your
pet best. Please read all nutritional information and safety warnings throughout
this book before giving your pets anything to eat.

To Paul and Michele: Thank you for showing me that life is always more enjoyable when you're surrounded by the people you love, good food, and a dog snoring under the table. My passion for entertaining stems from all of the hard work you poured into making every holiday magical for us. I love you so much. —Chris

To Mike and Jean: I carry your endless love and support with me every day. Thank you for making every occasion (even the smallest ones) special and memorable. I am the luckiest daughter and couldn't have asked for better parents. I love you! —Sarah

To Our Followers: You inspire us to be our best and to cherish every moment we have with our fur babies. We love you for allowing us to smile and laugh along with you. Thank you for always putting up with our shenanigans.

CONTENTS

INTRODUCTION

We've been told our entire lives that dogs should never be fed from the table, and you'd think that, over time, it has become easier to deny our corgis a tasty morsel whenever they give us a sweet look. Well, it hasn't. Our willpower is tested every time our pups cozy up next to us, whenever they hear the crinkle of a bag of chips, or when they find a comfortable spot next to our chairs at the dinner table.

Sarah and I have this constant desire to include our dogs, Hammy and Olivia, at our meals, whenever we gather around the table, but, sadly, we can only invite them to breathe the same air as us and watch us enjoy our food. This has never made sense to us. Our fondest memories are when our extended families gathered around the living room, indulging in appetizers, clinking glasses, and laughing so much that we forgot about the meal that we were cooking as it burned in the oven. Grabbing a yummy appetizer from the charcuterie board felt familial, and everyone in the room was welcome to reach over and dig in! We want to share memories like these with our furry companions and build charcuter—ahem . . . *barkcuterie* boards that include everything you know and love, but with treats that are perfect for your dog.

Hammy is a super-social butterfly who has an endearing passion for the culinary arts. In other words, he's my shadow in the kitchen! Whenever it's time to cook, he sports his own apron and hat because no dignified sous chef should be without them! Hammy's sophisticated palate has been the biggest inspiration for the dog-friendly boards your dog is about to enjoy. His spunky sister, Olivia, can be a very picky eater when she wants to be and very much prefers the finer things in life. Together, these two big personalities have come to life in these charming boards, perfect for celebrating a spring picnic in the park, Cinco de Mayo, a royally delightful afternoon teatime (Olivia's favorite), and, of course . . . your dog's birthday. These recipes and boards are healthy, easy to make, and customizable to your dog's taste buds!

As fur parents, we spend every free moment we have with our dogs. We cherish the time we have together because tomorrow is never guaranteed, and we like to make each day they get to spend with us special. Food has a funny way of strengthening that connection and creating a cute snack board is a wonderful way to do something special for the dog(s) in your life. We hope you get to make memories with your furry best friend that will last a lifetime.

—CHRIS, Dog Dad

NOTES ON INGREDIENTS

You can create your own dog-friendly spreads and snack trays with fresh fruit, vegetables, and a mix of homemade and store-bought treats. When shopping for ingredients, select organic and local items when possible. You can ensure the healthiest treats by using the best ingredients. The bonus of making your own treats is both knowing what your dog is eating and often spending less than on store-bought treats. The thirty-plus recipes in this book are a great place to start and easy to make.

KNOW YOUR DOG

Some pets have allergies to various ingredients. When feeding your dog a new treat, don't let them overindulge. Take note of their reaction. Just because an ingredient is safe for dogs, doesn't mean it will agree with your pet. For instance, some dogs are lactose intolerant and shouldn't be fed cheese or other dairy products. A lot of the recipes in this book are dairy-free, but some use yogurt and cheese. Dairy-free and/or gluten-free recipes are noted in the book with these icons:

SAFE AND HEALTHY FOODS FOR DOGS

The best foods for dogs are nutrient-rich or high in protein. Many fruits and vegetables are safe for dogs to eat and lean meats and peanut butter provide protein. The following foods are safe for dogs to eat.

Fruits

Apples
Bananas
Blueberries
Butternut squash
Cantaloupes
Kiwis
Mangos
Pears
Peaches
Pineapples
Pumpkin (cooked)
Strawberries

Vegetables

Asparagus
Bell peppers
Broccoli
Cabbage
Carrots
Cauliflower
Celery
Cucumbers
Lettuce
Peas
Sweet potatoes
Zucchini

Grains, Legumes, and Seeds

Brown rice
Carob
Chia seeds
Chickpea flour
Chickpeas
Flour (almond, gluten-free, oat, rice, whole wheat)
Lentils
Oatmeal
Peanut butter (unsweetened and creamy)
Peanuts
Popcorn

Meat, Seafood, and Dairy

Beef (lean)
Chicken (boneless and skinless)
Cottage cheese
Crab
Eggs
Pork (lean)
Salmon
Shrimp
Turkey
Yogurt

Natural Sweeteners

Honey
Maple syrup

SAFE FOODS FOR DOGS THAT SHOULD BE USED SPARINGLY

Many foods are safe for dogs to eat, but they should not be eaten in large quantities. Cheese is healthy for dairy-tolerant dogs, but too much can cause weight gain and other health problems. Simple carbohydrates, such as all-purpose flour, are also safe for dogs, but do not provide many nutrients, so should not be fed to dogs often. Use these ingredients sparingly. Food with any of these ingredients should be fed to your dog occasionally as treats—not as their main meal.

All-purpose flour
Coconut oil
Corn
Cheese
Milk

Leaveners (such as baking soda
    and baking powder)
Olive oil
Potatoes
Sunflower oil
White rice

FOODS THAT YOU SHOULD NEVER GIVE YOUR DOG

Some common foods consumed by people should never be given to dogs. These foods can be toxic for dogs and cause immediate or long-term health problems.

Alcohol
Artificial sweeteners
Avocados
Chocolate
Cocoa powder
Currants
Garlic
Grapes
Lemons

Limes
Macadamia nuts
Mushrooms
Onions
Pecans
Raisins
Salt (in high quantities)
Walnuts
Yeast dough

GETTING STARTED

You don't need much to get started making the boards and the recipes in this book and most likely you have a lot of the items. Though board or platter shapes are recommended, you can use any size, shape, and material of board you like, as it's more about artfully arranging the food items on the board for that perfect social media post . . . right before your dog excitedly destroys it. Here are some suggestions for equipment you may want to have on hand.

Supplies

These are suggested items for putting the boards together. You will see that not much is needed, as the food items are the most important part of creating each board. If you find that you really love making barkcuterie, you may want to invest in some canine-themed pieces.

Boards (various shapes, sizes, and materials)
Small and medium bowls
Small and medium ramekins
Medium and large cookie cutters (for themed boards)
Skewers
Balls
Ribbons
Festive garlands

Special Tools

These are suggested items for making the recipes beyond the basic kitchen tools you may already own, such as mixing bowls, mixing spoons, spatulas, baking sheets, parchment paper (or silicone baking mats), cooling rack, and so on.

Blender or food processor
Hand mixer
12-cup muffin pan (or two 6-cup pans)
Paper baking cups
12-cavity donut pan
Silicone molds (for themed boards)
12 ice pop molds
Small cookie cutters (for themed boards)
Letter cookie stamps
Cookie stamp
Round biscuit cutter
Disposable piping bags
Decorative piping tips

Spring
BOARDS

Easter Board

We may not agree on a lot of things, but we sure do love coordinating outfits and wearing our Easter finest, along with ears even bigger than our own. We created this board so that we can fuel up on some delicious treats before the big Easter egg hunt.

Board Items

Honeydew

Cantaloupe

Provolone cheese slices

Marbleized Easter Eggs (page 25)

Baby carrots

Carrot Pupcakes (page 22)

Three Dog Bakery Crunchy Itty Bitty Bones

Three Dog Bakery Lick'n Crunch! Golden & Vanilla Sandwich Cookies

Supplies

Rectangular tray with sides

Small egg- and flower-shaped cookie cutters

Bunny-shaped cookie cutter

Easter grass basket filler

Build Your Board

Slice the honeydew and cantaloupe ¾ inch (2 cm) thick. Using the small egg- and flower-shaped cookie cutters, create cutouts.

Cut out bunny shapes with the provolone cheese slices.

Fill the bottom third of the tray with Easter grass. Pile the Marbleized Easter Eggs on top of the grass. Center a stack of the bunny-shaped provolone above the Easter grass. Fill the area around the sides of the provolone with the baby carrots.

Line up the Carrot Pupcakes at the top of the tray. Create a row of honeydew and cantaloupe cutouts below the Pupcakes. Fill in remaining space with the Itty Bitty Bones and Sandwich Cookies.

CARROT PUPCAKES

Makes 10 pupcakes

Ingredients

PUPCAKES

2 large eggs

¼ cup (60 ml) melted coconut oil

¼ cup (60 ml) pure maple syrup

1½ cups (190 g) whole wheat flour

2 teaspoons baking powder

1 cup (110 g) shredded carrots, plus more for garnish (optional)

½ cup (120 ml) buttermilk

Dog-safe sprinkles, for garnish (optional)

FROSTING

1 package (8 ounces, or 226 g) cream cheese

1 tablespoon cornstarch

1 tablespoon pure maple syrup

Special Tools

12-cup muffin pan

10 paper baking cups

Disposable piping bag with decorating tip (optional)

1. **To make the pupcakes:** Preheat the oven to 375°F (190°C; gas mark 5). Line the muffin pan with the paper baking cups.

2. In a medium bowl, combine the eggs, oil, and ¼ cup (60 ml) syrup and mix until well combined. In a small bowl, stir together the flour and baking powder. Add the flour mixture to the egg mixture and mix just until combined. Stir in the carrots and buttermilk until fully incorporated. Fill each muffin cavity about three-quarters full with the batter.

3. Bake until lightly golden, 18 to 20 minutes. Let cool completely.

4. **Meanwhile, make the frosting:** In a medium bowl, combine the cream cheese, cornstarch, and 1 tablespoon syrup and beat until fluffy, 2 to 3 minutes.

5. When the pupcakes are completely cool, spread the frosting on them with an offset knife or the back of a spoon, or, if desired, use a disposable piping bag with a decorating tip to pipe the frosting onto the cakes. Garnish with dog-safe sprinkles or shredded carrots, if desired.

6. Store in an airtight container in the refrigerator for up to 5 days.

MARBLEIZED EASTER EGGS

Makes 12 eggs

Ingredients

12 large eggs

2 cups (480 ml) hot water

1 tablespoon white vinegar

Food coloring

3 cups (720 ml) water

¼ to ½ cup (60 to 120 ml) olive oil

1. Place the eggs in a medium pot and cover with water so that the water is 1 inch (2.5 cm) over the eggs. Bring the water to boil over high heat. As soon as the water starts to boil, turn off the heat and cover the pot. Let the eggs sit in the pot for 12 minutes. Drain the eggs and run cold water over them to stop them from cooking. Allow the eggs to cool completely before dyeing them.

2. Set a cooling rack on a baking sheet and set aside.

3. In a small bowl, mix the 2 cups (480 ml) hot water with the vinegar. Divide the hot water among 3 or 4 cups, then add 3 or 4 drops of desired food-coloring color to each cup for the base color of the eggs. Dip each egg in one of the cups. The longer the egg sits in the water the darker it will get. Place the dyed eggs on the prepared cooling rack. Let dry completely.

4. Divide the 3 cups (720 ml) water among 3 or 4 small bowls. Add 2 tablespoons olive oil to each bowl, then add 5 to 6 drops of food coloring to each bowl. Roll the solid-colored eggs in these colors—you can use more than one color. Place the marbleized eggs on the cooling rack. Let dry completely. Store the dried eggs in the refrigerator until ready to serve. Peel the shells from the hard-boiled eggs before feeding to your dog.

National Pet Day Board

APRIL 11

Though we created this board for dogs, we want to take this moment to also give a shout-out to all the non-canine pets. A lot of responsibility comes with being a pet and taking care of our humans, and we recognize all your kisses, cuddles, companionship, and enthusiasm. So, keep up the good work!

Board Items

Peanut Butter Biscuits
(page 29)

Banana Nut Donuts
(page 30)

Strawberries

Full Moon Natural Essentials
Jerky Tenders

Simply Nourish Soft Chews

Wiggles & Wags Bake Shop
PB & Yay

Supplies

Oval board

Ribbon

Build Your Board

Create four stacks of three Peanut Butter Biscuits each. Tie each stack with the ribbon and set aside.

Form a plus sign on your board with the Banana Nut Donuts.

Add a strawberry to each corner of the donut plus sign. Border the donuts with the Jerky Tenders and Soft Chews.

Add a tied biscuit stack to each corner of the board. Fill in remaining space with more Peanut Butter Biscuits and PB & Yay biscuits.

PEANUT BUTTER BISCUITS

Makes 30 biscuits

Ingredients

¾ cup (195 g) peanut butter

¼ cup (60 ml) unsalted chicken broth

1 large egg

1½ cups (180 g) whole wheat flour, plus more for dusting

Special Tools

Medium bone-shaped cookie cutter

1. Preheat the oven to 350°F (175°C; gas mark 4). Line a baking sheet with parchment paper or a silicone baking mat.

2. In a medium bowl, combine the peanut butter, broth, and egg and mix until well combined. Add the flour and mix just until incorporated and the mixture forms a soft dough.

3. On a lightly floured surface, roll out the dough to ½ inch (12 mm) thick with a rolling pin. Use the cookie cutter to cut out the cookies and transfer them to the prepared baking sheet.

4. Bake until golden brown, 20 to 25 minutes. Let cool completely.

5. Store in an airtight container for up to 1 week.

BANANA NUT DONUTS

Makes 12 donuts

Ingredients

DONUTS

Nonstick cooking spray

1 medium ripe banana, mashed

1 large egg

1 tablespoon melted coconut oil

1 tablespoon pure maple syrup

1½ cups (135 g) oat flour

1 tablespoon ground flax seeds

1 teaspoon baking powder

¼ cup (25 g) unsalted peanuts, finely chopped, for garnish

ICING

¼ cup (65 g) peanut butter

1 teaspoon honey

1 tablespoon cornstarch

Special Tools

12-cavity donut pan

Disposable piping bag (optional)

1. **To make the donuts:** Preheat the oven to 375°F (190°C; gas mark 5). Grease the donut cavities with nonstick cooking spray.

2. In a medium bowl, combine the banana, egg, oil, and syrup and mix until well combined. In a small bowl, stir together the flour, flax seeds, and baking powder. Add the flour mixture to the egg mixture and mix just until combined.

3. Scrape the batter into the disposable piping bag. Snip off the tip of the bag to create a 1-inch (2.5 cm) hole. Pipe the batter into the prepared pan, filling each cavity about three-quarters full.

4. Bake until golden brown, 10 to 14 minutes. Let the donuts cool in the pan for 5 minutes, then unmold and transfer to a cooling rack to cool completely.

5. **Meanwhile, make the icing:** Place the peanut butter and honey in a small heatproof bowl. Microwave on high for 20 seconds, then whisk to combine. The mixture should be thin enough to easily combine. If it is too thick, return the bowl to the microwave and heat for 10 more seconds, then whisk again. Whisk in the cornstarch. Using a knife, spread the icing onto the cooled donuts.

6. Store in an airtight container for up to 1 week.

Picnic Board

The perfect spring day calls for a picnic in the park! We love a good day of eating, playing, sunbathing, and, most importantly, dog watching. And we always make sure Dad brings our favorite blanket when we're ready for a well-deserved nap.

Board Items

Celery ribs, cut into 2- to 3-inch (5 to 7.5 cm) pieces, reserving the leaves

Peanut butter

Carrot Donuts (page 34)

Asparagus

Cheddar cheese slices

Colby Jack cheese slices

Deli turkey slices (thick cut)

Shredded carrot

Unsalted peanuts, finely chopped

Blueberries

Supplies

Rectangular board

Medium teardrop- and flower-shaped cookie cutters

Small flower-, butterfly-, and round-shaped cookie cutters

Build Your Board

Fill the celery pieces with peanut butter, then place on the bottom of the board for the ground.

Randomly place the Carrot Donuts on the board for flower centers. Place the asparagus as stems and the reserved celery leaves as leaves.

Cut out teardrops with cheddar, flowers with Colby Jack and cheddar, and butterflies and round shapes with turkey. Place the teardrops as flower petals. Fill in open spaces with flowers and butterflies. For the butterfly bodies, cut slivers of cheddar and Colby Jack and place on the butterflies. Use shredded carrot to form antennae. Place the turkey rounds on the larger cheese flowers, then garnish with chopped peanuts.

Place a blueberry in the center of each donut flower.

CARROT DONUTS

Makes 12 donuts

Ingredients

DONUTS

Nonstick cooking spray

2 large eggs

¼ cup (30 ml) sunflower oil

½ cup (125 g) unsweetened applesauce

1½ cups (190 g) whole wheat flour

1 teaspoon baking powder

¾ cup (85 g) finely shredded carrot, plus more for garnish

ICING

¼ cup (60 g) cream cheese

1 teaspoon pure maple syrup

1 tablespoon cornstarch

Special Tools

12-cavity donut pan

Disposable piping bag

1. **To make the donuts:** Preheat the oven to 375°F (190°C; gas mark 5). Grease the donut cavities with nonstick cooking spray.

2. In a medium bowl, combine the eggs, oil, and applesauce and mix until well combined. In a small bowl, stir together the flour and baking powder. Add the flour mixture to the egg mixture and mix just until combined. Stir in the shredded carrot.

3. Scrape the batter into the disposable piping bag. Snip off the tip of the bag to create a 1-inch (2.5 cm) hole. Pipe the batter into the prepared pan, filling each cavity about three-quarters full.

4. Bake until golden brown, 12 to 16 minutes. Let the donuts cool in the pan for 5 minutes, then unmold and transfer to a cooling rack to cool completely.

5. **Meanwhile make the icing:** Place the cream cheese and syrup in a small heatproof bowl. Microwave on high for 20 seconds, then whisk to combine. The mixture should be thin enough to easily combine. If it is too thick, return the bowl to the microwave and heat for 10 more seconds, then whisk again. Whisk in the cornstarch. Using a knife, spread the icing on the cooled donuts. Garnish with shredded carrot.

6. Store in an airtight container for up to 1 week.

Cinco de Mayo Platter

While some dogs are party animals, we're fiesta animals. We know that we really outdid ourselves with this board when the humans are even eyeing it. So, put on your sombreros, cue the mariachi band, and shake those tails!

Board Items

Low-sodium pinto beans, mashed to resemble refried beans

Fruit Salsa (page 39)

Frozen Cucumber Pawjitos (page 40)

Pineapple chunks

Seedless watermelon chunks

Full Moon Natural Essentials Jerky Tenders

Canine Carry Outs Taco Minis

SmartBones Churro Style Sticks

Queso fresco

Fresh cilantro

Fresh mint

Cucumber slices

Supplies

Large round platter

3 small bowls or ramekins

Skewers

Festive garland (optional)

Build Your Board

Place the three small bowls in the center of the platter. Fill one bowl with the mashed pinto beans, one with the Fruit Salsa, and reserve the last bowl for the Frozen Cucumber Pawjitos right before serving.

Make pineapple-watermelon kabobs by piercing the pineapple and watermelon chunks onto the skewers. Place them around the bowls on the platter. **(WARNING: When feeding to your dog, either remove the skewer and place the fruit in a bowl, or feed on the skewer, while making sure your dog doesn't eat the skewer.)**

Cut the Jerky Tenders into triangles to look like tortilla chips and place them near the salsa.

Fill in open spaces with Taco Minis and Churro Style Sticks. Add the Pawjitos to the third bowl right before serving. Garnish the pinto beans with some crumbled queso fresco and the platter with cilantro, mint, and cucumber slices. Add the festive garland to your table for more flare.

FRUIT SALSA

Makes 2 cups (320 g)

Ingredients

½ cup (85 g) chopped mango

½ cup (85 g) chopped pineapple

½ cup (75 g) chopped seedless watermelon

½ cup (75 g) chopped cucumber

1 tablespoon chopped fresh cilantro, plus more for garnish

1. Combine all the ingredients. Refrigerate until ready to serve.

2. Garnish with the fresh cilantro leaves.

FROZEN CUCUMBER PAWJITOS

Makes 15 to 20 pawjitos

Ingredients

1 small cucumber

10 fresh mint leaves

1 cup (240 ml) unsweetened
   coconut milk

½ cup (120 ml) water

1 tablespoon honey

Special Tools

Mini paw print-shaped
   silicone mold(s)

1. Cut the cucumber into ¼-inch-thick (6 mm) rounds. Cut each round in half so that it looks like a lime wedge. Set aside.

2. In a blender, process the mint, coconut milk, water, and honey until completely combined. Pour into the paw-shaped cavities, filling each one about ¼ inch (6 mm) from the top. Add a piece of cucumber to each mold. Freeze overnight or until solid.

3. Serve immediately after unmolding or store in an airtight container in the freezer for up to 1 month.

Summer
BOARDS

Take Your Dog to Work Day Board

JUNE 26

We deserve a raise with this board! I don't know why the humans are always complaining about work because when we show up to the office on this special day, the humans and dogs seem to be having lots of fun (and not doing much work).

Board Items

Apple Donuts (page 46)

Blueberries

Cauliflower florets

Broccoli florets

Full Moon Natural Essentials Jerky Tenders

Pork Chomps Crunchy Bones

Supplies

Rectangular board

Build Your Board

Create a circle of Apple Donuts in the center of the board.

Surround the donuts with a ring of blueberries, then surround the blueberries with a ring of cauliflower.

Place the broccoli florets at the top and bottom of the circle. Add the Jerky Tenders to the corners of the board, then fill in the top and bottom of the board with the Crunchy Bones.

APPLE DONUTS

Makes 12 donuts

Ingredients

DONUTS

Nonstick cooking spray

1 cup (250 g) unsweetened applesauce

1 large egg

½ cup (115 g) unsweetened plain yogurt

1 tablespoon melted coconut oil

1½ cups (188 g) whole wheat flour

1 teaspoon baking powder

Dog-safe sprinkles, for garnish (optional)

ICING

¼ package (2 ounces, or 60 g) cream cheese

1 tablespoon honey

1 tablespoon cornstarch

Dog-safe food coloring (optional)

Special Tools

12-cavity donut pan

Disposable piping bags

1. **To make the donuts:** Preheat the oven to 375°F (190°C; gas mark 5). Grease the donut cavities with nonstick cooking spray.

2. In a medium bowl, combine the applesauce, egg, yogurt, and oil and mix until well combined. In a small bowl, stir together the flour and baking powder. Add the flour mixture to the applesauce mixture and mix just until combined.

3. Scrape the batter into the disposable piping bag. Snip off the tip of the bag to create a 1-inch (2.5 cm) hole. Pipe the batter into the prepared pan, filling each cavity about three-quarters full.

4. Bake until golden brown, 18 to 20 minutes. Let the donuts cool in the pan for 5 minutes, then unmold and transfer to a cooling rack to cool completely.

5. **Meanwhile, make the icing:** Place the cream cheese and honey in a small heatproof bowl. Microwave on high for 20 seconds, then whisk to combine. The mixture should be thin enough to easily combine. If it is too thick, return the bowl to the microwave and heat for 10 more seconds, then whisk again. Whisk in the cornstarch, then stir in the food coloring, if using. Using a knife, spread the icing onto the cooled donuts. Garnish with sprinkles, if desired.

6. Store in an airtight container for up to 1 week.

Fourth of July Platter

JULY 4

We believe that the best Independence Day snack platter should look like an American flag and be as accurate as possible. That means fifty cheese stars! We tried to convince Dad of this, but he thought that was too much cheese. We're still working on it for next year, because it's all about going for the American dream, right?

Board Items

Full Moon Savory Sticks

Milk-Bone MaroSnacks

Blueberries

Provolone cheese slices

Red, White, and Blueberry Stars (page 51)

Supplies

White rectangular platter

Medium bowl, preferably blue

Small star-shaped cookie cutter

Build Your Board

Center the bowl near the top of the platter. Create three rows of red stripes with the Savory Sticks on the bottom half of the platter.

Create white stripes above and below the Savory Sticks with the MaroSnacks. Fill in the top portion of the platter around the bowl with blueberries.

Cut out star shapes from the provolone slices. Layer the cheese stars on top of the blueberries.

Add the Red, White, and Blueberry Stars to the bowl right before serving.

RED, WHITE, AND BLUEBERRY STARS

Makes 45 stars

Ingredients

½ cup (60 g) raspberries

½ cup (75 g) blueberries

1½ cups (345 g) unsweetened
   plain yogurt

1 tablespoon honey

Special Tools

Mini star-shaped silicone
   mold(s)

1. In a small bowl, mash the raspberries until mostly liquid and set aside. In a separate bowl, mash the blueberries until mostly liquid.

2. In a medium bowl, combine the yogurt and honey. Evenly divide the yogurt mixture among three small bowls.

3. With a rubber spatula, stir the mashed raspberries into one bowl of the yogurt mixture and the mashed blueberries into another bowl, leaving the remaining bowl plain. (For a marbleized look, do not overmix the raspberries and blueberries.)

4. Fill each star-shaped cavity three-quarters full with either the raspberry, blueberry, or plain mixture, making sure to have a variety of red, white, and blue colors. Freeze overnight or until solid.

5. Serve immediately after unmolding or store in an airtight container in the freezer for up to 1 month.

GF

National Dog Day Board

Host a party at the dog park or invite your doggy friends over for National Dog Day! We recommend having tug-o'-war, fetch, lots of space to run around, and this board. Cats are definitely allowed, especially if they're as friendly as Theodore. They can have some chicken biscuits, too, if only to knock them around a bit.

Board Items

Chicken Biscuits (page 54)

Celery slices

Colby Jack cheese slices, cut into bite-size squares

Apple slices

Claudia's Canine Bakery Spoil Me Baked Dog Treats

Pet by TASTY Biscuits

Supplies

Paw-shaped board

Build Your Board

Fill in the bottom portion of the board with the Chicken Biscuits, then layer the celery slices over the biscuits.

Add the cheese squares to one of the paw pads.

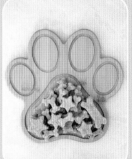

Fill in the remaining paw pads with the apple slices, Spoil Me Treats, and TASTY Biscuits.

CHICKEN BISCUITS

Makes 30 medium biscuits

Ingredients

1 cup (195 g) chopped boiled skinless, boneless chicken

1 large egg

½ cup (50 g) chopped celery

2 tablespoons melted coconut oil

1½ cups (190 g) whole wheat flour, plus more for dusting

Special Tools

Small and medium bone- and star-shaped cookie cutters

1. Preheat the oven to 350°F (175°C; gas mark 4). Line a baking sheet with parchment paper or a silicone baking mat.

2. Place the chicken, egg, celery, and oil in a food processor or blender and process until smooth. Transfer to a medium bowl. Add the flour and mix until incorporated and the mixture forms a soft dough.

3. On a lightly floured surface, roll out the dough to ½ inch (12 mm) thick. Use the cookie cutters to cut out the shapes and transfer them to the prepared baking sheet.

4. Bake until golden, 20 to 25 minutes. Let cool completely.

5. Store in an airtight container in the refrigerator for up to 5 days.

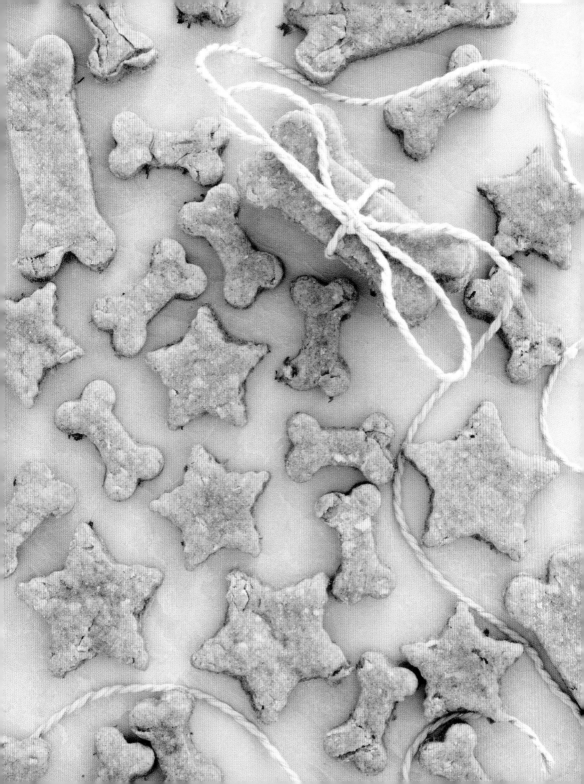

Beach Day Board

Sun's out, tongues out! There's nothing better than a relaxing beach or pool day. Hammy likes to splash around in the water while Olivia lazes under the umbrella. And though we look cool in our retro looks, we keep cool by eating pupsicles.

Board Items

Whole pineapple

Sliced and whole strawberries

Banana slices

Blueberries

Banana Berry Biscuits (page 60)

Wiggles & Wags Bake Shop Tropical Paradise Pineapple Cookie Tray

Three Dog Bakery Soft Baked Assort-Mutt Trio

Watermelon-Raspberry Pupsicles (page 63)

Supplies

Rectangular board

Cocktail umbrellas

Build Your Board

Cut the pineapple in half from top to bottom. Scoop out the core and some of the fruit of one of the halves to form a bowl. Center it on the board.

Mix together the sliced strawberries, bananas, and blueberries in the pineapple bowl.

Place the Banana Berry Biscuits around the board. Fill in open areas with the Tropical Paradise Cookies, Assort-Mutt Trio, whole strawberries, and more blueberries, leaving space for the Watermelon-Raspberry Pupsicles.

Add the Pupsicles right before serving. Stick some cocktail umbrellas into the pineapple to decorate. **(WARNING: Remove the cocktail umbrellas before sharing the board with your dog so that they don't accidentally eat one and possibly get injured.)**

BANANA BERRY BISCUITS

Makes 20 to 25 biscuits

Ingredients

2 cups (250 g) whole wheat flour, plus more for dusting

½ cup (45 g) rolled oats

1 tablespoon ground flax seeds

1 medium ripe banana

3 strawberries

½ cup (125 g) unsweetened applesauce

1 recipe Doggie Royal Icing (opposite)

Special Tools

Mini summer-themed cookie cutters

1. Preheat the oven to 350°F (175°C; gas mark 4). Line a baking sheet with parchment paper or a silicone baking mat.

2. In a medium bowl, stir together the flour, oats, and flax seeds; set aside.

3. Place the banana, strawberries, and applesauce in a blender and process until smooth. Add the banana mixture to the bowl with the flour mixture and mix until incorporated and the mixture forms a soft dough.

4. On a lightly floured surface, roll out the dough to ¼ inch (6 mm) thick. Use the cookie cutters to cut out the shapes and transfer them to the prepared baking sheet.

5. Bake until golden brown, 20 to 25 minutes. Let cool completely.

6. Pipe designs onto the biscuits with the Doggie Royal Icing.

7. Store in an airtight container for up to 3 days.

DOGGIE ROYAL ICING

Makes about 3/4 cup (180 mL)

Ingredients

3 tablespoons water

1 tablespoon pasturized egg white powder

2 tablespoons cream cheese, softened

1 tablespoon honey

¼ cup (30 g) cornstarch, plus more if needed

Dog-safe food coloring

Special Tools

Disposable piping bags

1. Using an electric mixer with the whisk attachment, beat the water and egg white powder until foamy. Add the cream cheese and honey and beat until smooth. Add the cornstarch and beat until smooth. If the mixture is too runny add more cornstarch, one teaspoon at a time, until desired consistency is reached.

2. Divide the frosting into separate bowls depending on the number of colors you prefer. Mix in the food coloring, then transfer the icing to the disposable piping bags. Cut a very small hole at the tip of each bag.

NOTE: If using more than two colors, you may need to double the recipe.

WATERMELON-RASPBERRY PUPSICLES

Makes 12 pupsicles

Ingredients

1½ cups (225 g) cubed seedless watermelon

½ cup (60 g) raspberries

2 cups (460 g) unsweetened plain yogurt

1 tablespoon honey

Special Tools

12 ice pop molds (3 ounces, or 90 ml, each)

12 wood Popsicle sticks

1. In a shallow bowl, mash the watermelon and raspberries into a chunky purée.

2. In a medium bowl, combine the yogurt and honey.

3. With a rubber spatula, stir the watermelon mixture into the yogurt mixture. (For a marbleized look, do not overmix; for pink ice pops, stir until completely combined.)

4. Evenly divide the mixture among the ice pop molds. Place the covers on the molds and insert the Popsicle sticks. Freeze overnight or until solid. **(WARNING: When feeding to your dog, either remove the stick and place the ice pop in a bowl, or feed on the stick, while making sure your dog doesn't eat the stick.)**

5. Store in an airtight container in the freezer for up to 1 month.

Autumn
BOARDS

Park Day Board

Being naturally cozy creatures, we love donning our flannels, sweaters, scarves, and hats and going to the park on a crisp autumn day. After jumping in and out of piles of leaves, there's nothing better than indulging in our favorite fall flavors.

Board Items

Pumpkin and Apple Pupcakes (page 68)

Red, orange, and yellow bell pepper slices

Maple Oatmeal Biscuits (page 71)

Three Dog Bakery Lick'n Crunch! Carob & Peanut Butter Sandwich Cookies

Twistix Peanut Butter and Carob Dental Dog Treats

Fruitables Skinny Minis Pumpkin & Berry Flavor Soft & Chewy Dog Treats

Supplies

Rectangular board

Build Your Board

Place a row of Pumpkin and Apple Pupcakes on the top and bottom of the board.

Lay a row of the bell pepper slices across the center of the board, creating an ombré effect.

Lay a row of alternating stacked Maple Oatmeal Biscuits and Carob & Peanut Butter Sandwich Cookies above and below the bell pepper slices.

Lay the Twistix on the edges between the Pupcakes and the Biscuits and Sandwich Cookies. Fill in the space between the Twistix with the Fruitables.

PUMPKIN AND APPLE PUPCAKES

Makes 12 pupcakes

Ingredients

PUPCAKES

1 cup (245 g) canned pure pumpkin (not pumpkin pie mix)

½ cup (125 g) unsweetened applesauce

¼ cup (60 ml) pure maple syrup

2 large eggs

¼ cup (60 ml) sunflower oil

2 cups (250 g) whole wheat flour

½ teaspoon ground cinnamon

1 teaspoon baking powder

Dog-safe sprinkles, for garnish (optional)

FROSTING

1 package (8 ounces, or 227 g) cream cheese, softened

1 tablespoon tapioca flour

1 tablespoon pure maple syrup

Dog-safe food coloring (optional)

Special Tools

12-cup muffin pan

12 paper baking cups

Disposable piping bag with decorator tip (optional)

1. **To make the pupcakes:** Preheat the oven to 350°F (175°C; gas mark 4). Line the muffin pan with the paper baking cups.

2. In a medium bowl, combine the pumpkin, applesauce, ¼ cup (60 ml) syrup, eggs, and oil and mix until smooth. In a small bowl, stir together the flour, cinnamon, and baking powder. Add the flour mixture to the egg mixture and mix just until combined. Fill each muffin cavity about three-quarters full with the batter.

3. Bake until lightly golden, 18 to 22 minutes. Let cool completely.

4. **Meanwhile, make the frosting:** In a medium bowl, combine the cream cheese, flour, and 1 tablespoon syrup and beat until fluffy, 2 to 3 minutes. Stir in the food coloring, if using.

5. When the pupcakes are completely cool, spread the frosting on them with an offset knife or the back of a spoon, or, if desired, use a disposable piping bag with a decorator tip to pipe the frosting onto the cakes.

6. Store in an airtight container in the refrigerator for up to 5 days.

MAPLE OATMEAL BISCUITS

Makes 40 biscuits

Ingredients

½ cup (115 g) unsweetened plain yogurt

¼ cup (60 ml) pure maple syrup

1 large egg

½ cup (45 g) rolled oats

2 cups (180 g) oat flour, plus more for dusting

Special Tools

Small maple leaf–shaped cookie cutter

1. Preheat the oven to 350°F (175°C; gas mark 4). Line a baking sheet with parchment paper or a silicone baking mat.

2. In a medium bowl, combine the yogurt, syrup, and egg and mix until well combined. Add the oats and oat flour and mix just until incorporated and the mixture forms soft dough.

3. On a lightly floured surface, roll out the dough to ½ inch (12 mm) thick. Use the cookie cutter to cut out the shapes and transfer them to the prepared baking sheet.

4. Bake until golden, 15 to 18 minutes. Let cool completely.

5. Store in an airtight container for up to 1 week.

Oktoberfest Board

We refuse to wear a dirndl and lederhosen for Oktoberfest. Why, you ask? Because they're kind of tight, and we need room for our stomachs to expand while we eat all our favorite German-style treats. Now, Theodore in lederhosen is an adorable sight.

Board Items

Pwetzels (page 75)

Kale leaves

Three Dog Bakery Lick'n Crunch! Carob & Peanut Butter Sandwich Cookies

Snausages In a Blanket

Milo's Kitchen Beef Sausage Slices with Rice

Thrills & Chills Halloween Gourdgeous Cookie

Three Dog Bakery Soft Baked Pumpkin Woofers

Supplies

Rectangular board

Build Your Board

Line three Pwetzels down the center of the board and place one in each corner.

Place the kale below the Pwetzels in the top corners and above the Pwetzels in the bottom corners.

Place a stack of Carob & Peanut Butter Sandwich Cookies on the center of each side of the board.

Fill in the open space between the kale and center Pwetzels with Snausages.

Fill in the open space on the top of the board with Beef Sausage Slices.

Center the Halloween Gourdgeous Cookie on the bottom of the board, then fill in open spaces with Pumpkin Woofers.

PWETZELS

Makes 8 pwetzels

Ingredients

2 large eggs, divided

1 cup (328 g) cooked, mashed sweet potato

1 tablespoon sunflower oil

1½ cups (250 g) whole wheat flour, plus more as needed and for dusting

¼ cup (40 g) sesame seeds

1. Preheat the oven to 350°F (175°C; gas mark 4). Line a baking sheet with parchment or a silicone baking mat.

2. Separate one of the eggs; put the white in a medium bowl and the yolk in a small bowl. Beat the yolk with a fork and set aside.

3. Add the mashed sweet potato, the remaining whole egg, and the oil to the bowl with the egg white. While mixing, add the flour, a little at a time, until the mixture forms a soft dough that is not sticky to the touch. (You may need more or less flour depending on the amount of moisture.) Divide the dough into 8 equal portions and form each one into a ball.

4. On a lightly floured surface, roll each dough ball into a rope, about 10 inches (25 cm) long. With a hand holding each end of the rope, pull the ends away from you, then twist them around each other about 1 inch (2.5 cm) from the ends to create a loop at the bottom. Fold the twisted half over the lower loop and attach the ends to the center of the loop to form a pretzel shape. Place on the prepared baking sheet. Repeat with the remaining dough balls.

5. Brush the pwetzels with the beaten egg yolk and sprinkle with the sesame seeds. Bake until golden brown, 20 to 25 minutes.

Halloween Board

OCTOBER 31

Trick or treat! With our penchant for dressing up, we like to live every day as Halloween, but we never pass up the opportunity to participate in a Halloween dog parade. It's not about winning a prize but seeing all our friends dressed in the most adorable costumes. And there's nothing better than sharing this spookily delicious board with them.

Board Items

Carob Pumpkin Biscuits (page 80)

Thrills & Chills Halloween Creepin' It Real Chews

Kiwi slices

Blackberries

Thrills & Chills Halloween Groans & Bones Cookies

Milk-Bone Spooky Biscuits

Thrills & Chills Halloween Boo-Tiful Buffet Cookie Tray

Supplies

Rectangular tray with sides

Festive garland (optional)

Build Your Board

Drape the festive garland around the tray, if you like.

Center three stacks of the Carob Pumpkin Biscuits in the center of the tray.

Add a Creepin' It Real Chew to each corner. Fill in the space between the Chews with the kiwi slices.

Add a row of blackberries below and above the kiwi slices. Add a row of Groans & Bones Cookies above and below the blackberries.

Fill in the open space around the Carob Pumpkin Biscuits with the Spooky Biscuits and the small Boo-Tiful Buffet Cookies. Top each row of blackberries with a paw-shaped Boo-Tiful Buffet Cookie.

CAROB PUMPKIN BISCUITS

Makes 15 large biscuits

Ingredients

BISCUITS

1 cup (245 g) canned pure pumpkin (not pumpkin pie mix)

¼ cup (65 g) unsweetened almond butter

2 large eggs

2 cups (180 g) oat flour

1 cup (115 g) almond flour, plus more for dusting

GLAZE

4 ounces (113 g) carob chips

1 tablespoon sunflower oil

Special Tools

Large bone-shaped cookie cutter

1. **To make the biscuits:** Preheat the oven to 350°F (175°C; gas mark 4). Line a baking sheet with parchment paper or a silicone baking mat. Set a cooling rack over a sheet of parchment paper.

2. In a medium bowl, combine the pumpkin, almond butter, and eggs and mix until well combined. Add the flour and mix until incorporated and the mixture forms a soft dough.

3. On a lightly floured surface, roll out the dough to ½ inch (12 mm) thick. Use the cookie cutter to cut out the shapes and transfer them to the prepared baking sheet.

4. Bake for 20 to 25 minutes. Let cool completely.

5. **Meanwhile, make the glaze:** Fill the bottom part of a double boiler with water and bring to a simmer over medium-high heat. Put the carob chips and oil in the top part of the double boiler and stir constantly until smooth.

6. When the biscuits have cooled completely, transfer them to the prepared cooling rack and drizzle the glaze over them, letting the excess glaze drip onto the parchment paper underneath. Let the glaze set before serving or storing.

7. Store in an airtight container for up to 1 week.

Thanksgiving Board

The day humans call Thanksgiving, we call National Dog Show Day! We love seeing all the different breeds strutting their stuff, but of course, we're rooting for the corgi. That said, we won't turn down a Thanksgiving feast!

Board Items

Green beans, lightly steamed

Carrots, lightly steamed

Deli turkey slices

Colby Jack cheese slices

Mashed sweet potatoes

Cranberry sauce

Fall Bites (page 84)

Rachael Ray Nutrish Turkey Bites

BLUE Nudges Homestyle Chicken Pot Pie Natural Dog Treats

BLUE Wilderness Trail Treats Turkey Grain-Free Biscuits

Fruitables Crispy Bacon & Apple Flavor

Supplies

Rectangular tray with sides

Medium shallow bowl

2 small bowls or ramekins

Skewers or toothpicks

Build Your Board

Place the steamed veggies in the shallow bowl and place the bowl in the center of the tray.

Roll up the turkey and Colby Jack slices together and secure with skewers. Layer some roll-ups at the top right and bottom left of the bowl. **(WARNING: When feeding to your dog, either remove the skewer and place the food in a bowl, or feed on the skewer, while making sure they don't eat the skewer.)**

Fill one of the small bowls with the mashed sweet potatoes and the other with the cranberry sauce. Place the sweet potatoes at the bottom right of the shallow bowl and the cranberries at the top left.

Fill in the area between the cranberry sauce and roll-ups with the Fall Bites. Fill in around the shallow bowl with the Turkey Bites and Nudges Pot Pies. Fill in the corners of the tray with the Turkey Biscuits and Fruitables on opposite sides.

FALL BITES

Makes 40 bites

Ingredients

1 cup (195 g) shredded cooked low-sodium turkey

¼ cup (35 g) dried cranberries

½ cup (125 g) unsweetened applesauce

¼ cup (60 ml) pure maple syrup

1 large egg

1½ cups (190 g) whole wheat flour

Special Tools

Cookie stamp or glass

1. Preheat the oven to 350°F (175°C; gas mark 4). Line a baking sheet with parchment paper or a silicone baking mat.

2. Place the turkey, cranberries, applesauce, syrup, and egg in a food processor or blender. Process until smooth and transfer to a medium bowl. Add the flour and mix until a soft dough forms.

3. Form the dough into ¾-inch (2 cm) balls. Press the balls with a cookie stamp (or if you don't have one, use the bottom of a glass), flattening them to about ⅓ inch (8.5 mm) thick. Carefully peel the pressed cookies off the cookie press and carefully transfer to the prepared baking sheet.

4. Bake until golden, 10 to 12 minutes. Let cool completely.

5. Store in an airtight container in the refrigerator for up to 5 days.

Winter
BOARDS

Christmas Board

DECEMBER 25

Merry Christmas! We have put together all our holiday favorites for grazing by the Christmas tree while we open our presents. Just in case Santa has dogs, we left some of our favorite homemade biscuits for them. We bet the reindeer will like them too!

Board Items

Strawberries

Raspberries

Kale leaves

Gingerbread Biscuits (page 90)

Santa Paws (page 93)

Nutri Chomps Chicken Twist

Premium Mini Pork Chomps Bacon Flavor Twists

Buddy Biscuits Original Oven Baked with Peanut Butter

Wiggles & Wags Bake Shop Incredi Bears

Supplies

Round board

Festive ribbon

Build Your Board

Center the berries on the board and surround them with the kale.

Make two stacks of three or four Gingerbread Biscuits. Tie each stack with the ribbon, then place one stack at the top right of the berries and kale and the other at the bottom left.

Artfully arrange more Gingerbread Biscuits, the Santa Paws, and the store-bought treats to fill the remaining open space.

GINGERBREAD BISCUITS

Makes 15 to 20 biscuits

Ingredients

½ cup (125 g) unsweetened applesauce

1 large egg

2 tablespoons (30 ml) unsulfured molasses

1¾ cups (438 g) whole wheat flour, plus more for dusting

¼ teaspoon ground cinnamon

½ teaspoon ginger powder

½ teaspoon baking soda

1 recipe Doggie Royal Icing (page 61)

Special Tools

Medium bone- and snowflake-shaped cookie cutters

1. Preheat the oven to 350°F (175°C; gas mark 4). Line a baking sheet with parchment paper or a silicone baking mat.

2. In a medium bowl, combine the applesauce, egg, and molasses and mix until well combined. In a small bowl, combine the flour, cinnamon, ginger powder, and baking soda. Add the flour mixture to the applesauce mixture and mix until incorporated and the mixture forms a soft dough.

3. On a lightly floured surface, roll out the dough to ¼ inch (6 mm) thick with a rolling pin. Use the cookie cutters to cut out the shapes and transfer them to the prepared baking sheet.

4. Bake for 15 to 20 minutes. Let cool completely.

5. Pipe designs onto the biscuits with the Doggie Royal Icing. Let the icing set before serving or storing.

6. Store in an airtight container in the refrigerator for up to 1 week.

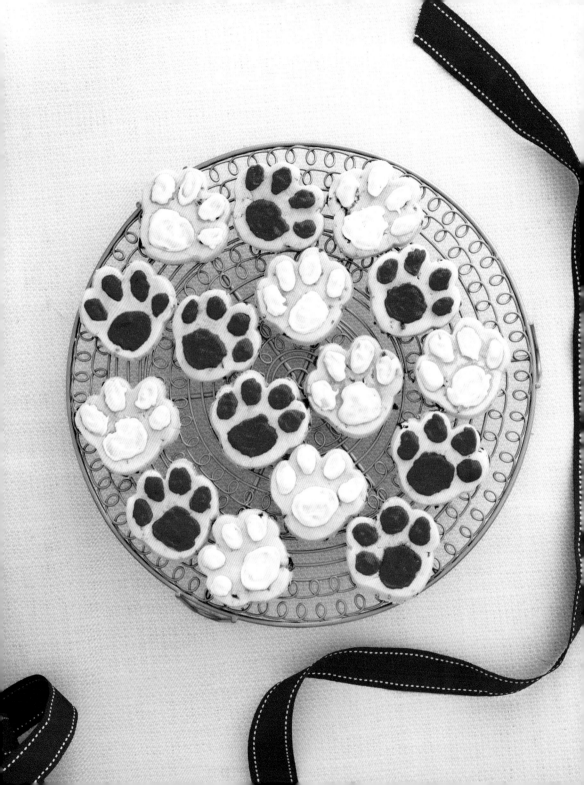

SANTA PAWS

Makes about 20 paws

Ingredients

¼ cup (35 g) dried cranberries

10 to 12 fresh mint leaves

½ cup (115 g) unsweetened plain yogurt

½ cup (120 ml) unsalted chicken broth

1¾ cups (235 g) gluten-free flour, plus more for dusting

1 recipe Doggie Royal Icing (page 61)

Special Tools

Medium paw-shaped cookie cutter

1. Preheat the oven to 350°F (175°C; gas mark 4). Line a baking sheet with parchment paper or a silicone baking mat.

2. In a food processer, finely chop the cranberries and mint.

3. In a medium bowl mix the yogurt, broth, and cranberry-mint mixture until well combined. Add the flour and mix just until combined.

4. On a lightly floured surface, roll out the dough to ¼ inch (6 mm) thick with a rolling pin. Use the cookie cutter to cut out the shapes and carefully transfer them to the prepared baking sheet.

5. Bake for 15 to 20 minutes or until they start to darken at the edges. Let cool completely.

6. Pipe designs onto the paws with the Doggie Royal Icing. Let the icing set before serving or storing.

7. Store in an airtight container for up to 1 week.

New Year's Eve Board

Happy New Year! Not only do we get to wear our favorite party clothes, but we also get to stay up past our bedtime. And when the clock strikes midnight, we share lots of sloppy kisses while barking at the top of our lungs to "Auld Lang Syne." Cheers to another year of adventure, fun, and our favorite treats!

Board Items

- Peanut Butter Cream Cheese Ball (page 96)
- Celery sticks
- Carrot sticks
- Broccoli florets
- Apple slices
- Cheese Sticks (page 99)
- Simply Nourish Soft Chews
- Three Dog Bakery Soft Baked Assort-Mutt Trio
- Pet by TASTY Biscuits
- Three Dog Bakery Celebration Confetti

Supplies

Rectangular board

Build Your Board

Center the Peanut Butter Cream Cheese Ball on the board. Flank the ball with the celery and carrot sticks. Fill in the remaining sides with the broccoli florets, then layer the apple slices over the celery and carrots.

Lay the Cheese Sticks across the top and bottom of the board. Frame the sides of the board with the Soft Chews.

Fill in the corners of the board with the Assort-Mutt Trio and TASTY Biscuits.

Fill in any open space with the Celebration Confetti.

PEANUT BUTTER CREAM CHEESE BALL

Serves 15

Ingredients

¼ cup (25 g) unsalted peanuts

2 store-bought peanut butter–flavored dog biscuits

¼ cup (35 g) dog-safe sprinkles

½ package (4 ounces, or 113 g) cream cheese, softened

¾ cup (195 g) peanut butter

½ cup (45 g) oat flour

1. Place the peanuts and dog biscuits in a food processor. Pulse until finely chopped and transfer to a shallow bowl. Stir in the sprinkles and set aside.

2. In a medium bowl, combine the cream cheese, peanut butter, and flour and mix until well combined.

3. Place the mixture on parchment paper and form into a ball. Roll the ball in the peanut mixture. Wrap in parchment paper and refrigerate for 2 to 3 hours before serving.

4. Store in an airtight container in the refrigerator for up to 1 week.

CHEESE STICKS

Makes 9 sticks

Ingredients

3 large eggs, divided

½ cup (55 g) shredded cheddar cheese, plus more for sprinkling

¼ cup (65 g) unsweetened applesauce

1¾ cups (230 g) whole wheat flour, plus more for dusting

1. Preheat the oven to 375°F (190°C; gas mark 5). Line a baking sheet with parchment paper or a silicone baking mat.

2. In a small bowl, beat 1 egg for an egg wash and set aside.

3. In a medium bowl, combine the cheese, remaining 2 eggs, applesauce, and flour and mix until well combined and the mixture forms a soft dough.

4. On a lightly floured surface, roll out the dough to a rough 6 x 14-inch (15 x 36 cm) rectangle with a rolling pin. Brush with some of the egg wash. Sprinkle with more cheese, then press the cheese into the dough so that it sticks. Carefully flip the rectangle over and repeat with the egg wash and cheese.

5. Cut the dough rectangle into 1½-inch-wide (4 cm) strips off the short side. Twist about 4 times to create a corkscrew shape. Arrange them on the prepared baking sheet.

6. Bake until golden, 18 to 22 minutes. Let cool completely.

7. Store in an airtight container in the refrigerator for up to 5 days.

Valentine's Day Board

FEBRUARY 14

Happy Valentine's Day! We hope everyone likes our handmade cards that we signed with our paw prints. (We made quite the mess . . . paw prints around the house for days!) And we hope your dogs feel all the love with this special board we made from our hearts.

Board Items

Raspberries

Red bell pepper slices

Strawberries

Pork Chomps Crunchy Bones

Ark Naturals Softshield Protection+ Dental Chews

Wiggles & Wags Bake Shop Incredi Bears

Raspberry Biscuits (page 103)

Wiggles & Wags Bake Shop PB & Yay

BLUE Bits Tender Beef Training Treats

Sweet Melon Bites (page 104)

Supplies

Rectangular board

Small shallow bowl

Large heart-shaped cookie cutter

Red ribbon

Build Your Board

Center the cookie cutter and bowl on the board. Fill the cookie cutter with the raspberries.

Lay most of the bell pepper slices, angling down, between the cookie cutter and bowl.

Place a strawberry on the end of each bell pepper group. Place a strawberry on the top center of the board and frame it with bell pepper slices in a heart shape.

Angle a Crunchy Bone from each top corner, then fill in the areas between the Crunchy Bones and the strawberry heart with the Softshield Protection+ Chews.

Stack a couple of Crunchy Bones, tie the ribbon around them, and place on the bottom center of the board. Fill in the area at the bottom of the board with the Incredi Bears.

Fill in open spaces with the Raspberry Biscuits, PB & Yay biscuits, and BLUE Bits. Add the Sweet Melon Bites to the bowl right before serving.

RASPBERRY BISCUITS

Makes about 50 small hearts

Ingredients

BISCUITS
½ cup (60 g) raspberries

¼ cup (60 ml) coconut oil

1 egg

1¾ cups (160 g) oat flour, plus more for dusting

GLAZE
2 tablespoons water

1 tablespoon honey

¼ cup (30 g) cornstarch

Equipment

Small heart-shaped cookie cutter

1. **To make the biscuits:** Preheat the oven to 350°F (175°C; gas mark 4). Line a baking sheet with parchment paper or a silicone baking mat. Set a cooling rack over a sheet of parchment paper.

2. In a medium bowl, mix the raspberries, coconut oil, and egg until the raspberries have broken down and the ingredients are well combined. Add the flour and mix just until combined.

3. On a lightly floured surface, roll out the dough to ¼ inch (6 mm) thick. Use the cookie cutter to cut out the shapes and transfer them to the prepared baking sheet.

4. Bake until the biscuits start to brown at the edges, 15 to 20 minutes. Let cool completely.

5. **Meanwhile, make the glaze:** In a small bowl, whisk together the water, honey, and cornstarch until well combined.

6. When the biscuits have cooled completely, transfer them to the prepared cooling rack and drizzle the glaze over them, letting the excess glaze drip onto the parchment paper underneath. Let the drizzle set before serving or storing.

7. Store in an airtight container for up to 1 week.

SWEET MELON BITES

About 50 hearts

Ingredients

1½ cups (225 g) cubed seedless
  watermelon
1 cup (240 ml) unsweetened
  coconut milk
1 tablespoon honey

Equipment

Mini heart-shaped silicone
  mold(s)

1. Place all the ingredients in a blender and process until smooth.

2. Fill the heart-shaped cavities with the mixture. Freeze overnight or until solid.

3. Unmold and serve immediately or store in an airtight container in the freezer for up to 1 month.

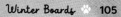

National Dog Biscuit Day Board

It's our favorite holiday of the year! And we need all the biscuits—big and small, sweet and savory, thin and thick, homemade and store-bought—to celebrate. We can guarantee that no biscuit will be left behind.

Board Items

Peanut butter

Honey

Apple slices

Apple Chia Seed Biscuits (page 109)

Old Mother Hubbard Classic Bac'N'Cheez Biscuits

Old Mother Hubbard Classic Mini Mix

Three Dog Bakery Soft Baked Peanut Butter & Banana Woofers

Supplies

Dog bone–shaped board

Small ramekin

Build Your Board

Fill the ramekin with the peanut butter and top with about a teaspoon of the honey. Center the ramekin on the board.

Place the apple slices above and below the ramekin.

Fill in the rest of the board with the Apple Chia Seed Biscuits and store-bought treats.

APPLE CHIA SEED BISCUITS

Makes 25 to 30 biscuits

Ingredients

½ cup (125 g) unsweetened applesauce

¼ cup (60 ml) melted coconut oil

1 large egg

1 tablespoon chia seeds

1¾ cups (220 g) whole wheat flour, plus more for dusting

Equipment

Small bone- and dog-shaped cookie cutters

Letter cookie stamps (optional)

1. Preheat the oven to 325°F (165°F; gas mark 3). Line a baking sheet with parchment paper or a silicone baking mat.

2. In a medium bowl, combine the applesauce, coconut oil, and egg and mix until well combined. Add the chia seeds and flour and mix until incorporated and the mixture forms a soft dough.

3. On a lightly floured surface, roll out the dough to ½ inch (12 mm) thick. Use the cookie cutters to cut out the shapes and transfer them to the prepared baking sheet. (For extra flair, you can stamp your pup's name or a fun message with the letter cookie stamps.)

4. Bake until golden, 20 to 25 minutes. Let cool completely.

5. Store in an airtight container for up to 1 week.

St. Patrick's Day Board

Kiss us, we're Irish! Well, actually, we're Welsh, but we hear that Wales and Ireland are pretty close to each other. After we enjoy our green treats, we're going to put on our detective hats and search for the pot o' gold with the help of Theodore. We've all agreed that the money will be spent on more treats.

Board Items

Honeydew

Kale

Savoy cabbage

Mint and Cabbage Shamrock Biscuits (page 115)

Bocce's Bakery Market Greens Biscuits

VetIQ Minties Dental Bone

Three Dog Bakery Lick'n Crunch! Golden & Vanilla Sandwich Cookies

Fresh mint leaves

Supplies

Square tray with sides

Small shamrock-shaped cookie cutter

Build Your Board

Slice the honeydew ¾ inch (2 cm) thick. Using the cookie cutter, create cutouts.

Lay a bed of the kale and cabbage in your tray.

Artfully arrange the Mint and Cabbage Shamrock Biscuits, honeydew shamrocks, and store-bought treats on top of the kale and cabbage.

Garnish with the fresh mint leaves.

MINT AND CABBAGE SHAMROCK BISCUITS

Makes about 30 shamrocks

Ingredients

½ cup (35 g) chopped green cabbage

¼ cup (50 g) fresh mint leaves

¼ cup (60 ml) water

2 tablespoons honey

1 large egg

1 cup (115 g) almond flour

1 cup (90 g) oat flour, plus more for dusting

Equipment

Small shamrock-shaped cookie cutter

1. Preheat the oven to 350°F (175°C; gas mark 4). Line a baking sheet with parchment paper or a silicone baking mat.

2. Place the cabbage, mint, and water in a blender and process until smooth. Transfer to a medium bowl.

3. Add the honey and egg and mix until well combined. Add the flours and mix until incorporated and the mixture forms a soft dough.

4. On a lightly floured surface, roll out the dough to ½ inch (12 mm) thick. Use the cookie cutter to cut out the shapes and transfer them to the prepared baking sheet.

5. Bake until golden around the edges, 20 to 25 minutes. Let cool completely.

6. Store in an airtight container for up to 1 week.

Anytime
BOARDS

Teatime Board

Don't worry, we haven't turned posh! But we did want to honor our Welsh heritage with a tea party. We'll admit that this board is probably not fit for royalty, but the royal corgis would be fans.

Board Items

Dog-safe tea or chicken broth

Cucumber and Cream Cheese Sandwiches (page 121)

Doggie Scones (page 122)

Raspberry Jam (page 123)

Clotted cream

Raspberries

Peaches

Three Dog Bakery Lick'n Crunch! Golden & Vanilla Sandwich Cookies

Wiggles & Wags Bake Shop Short & Sweet

Wiggles & Wags Bake Shop Chip, Chip Hooray

Wiggles & Wags Bake Shop Paw Print Cookie

Supplies

Rectangular tray with sides

Teapot

2 teacups and saucers

2 dessert plates

2 small bowls or ramekins

Build Your Board

Set the teapot in the center of the tray. Place the teacups and saucers around the teapot and fill the teacups with tea or chicken broth.

Set the dessert plates in the tray at opposite corners. Place the Cucumber and Cream Cheese Sandwiches on one of the plates and the Doggie Scones on the other.

Fill the small bowls with the Raspberry Jam and clotted cream, then place the bowls near the plate with the Scones.

Fill in the remaining space with the fruit and store-bought cookie treats.

CUCUMBER AND CREAM CHEESE SANDWICHES

Makes 6 sandwiches

Ingredients

1 medium cucumber

6 slices whole wheat sandwich bread

½ package (4 ounces, or 113 g) cream cheese, softened

Special Tools

Vegetable or potato peeler

Medium bone-shaped cookie cutter

1. Using the peeler, peel strips down the sides of the cucumber, creating a striped look. Slice the cucumber into 6 thin rounds, then cut each round in half.

2. Use the cookie cutter to cut out 2 bone shapes per each slice of bread.

3. Spread some cream cheese on each bread bone. Place 2 cucumber slices each on half of the bread bones and top with the remaining bread bones.

4. Serve immediately or store in an airtight container in the refrigerator for up to 1 day.

DOGGIE SCONES

Makes 10 scones

Ingredients

1 cup (125 g) self-rising flour

½ cup (45 g) oat flour, plus more for dusting

¼ cup (60 g) vegan butter (not avocado)

2 tablespoons honey

¼ cup (60 ml) milk

1 egg, beaten

Special Tools

Round biscuit cutter

1. Preheat the oven to 350°F (175°C; gas mark 4).

2. In a medium bowl, stir together the flours. Cut the butter into small pieces and add it to the flour. Continue cutting the butter until a crumb forms.

3. Add the honey and milk and mix just until the dough comes together.

4. On a lightly floured surface, roll out the dough to ½ inch (12 mm) thick. Cut out shapes with the biscuit cutter and transfer to a baking sheet. Brush the tops with the beaten egg.

5. Bake until golden, 20 to 25 minutes. Let cool completely.

6. Store in an airtight container for up to 1 week.

RASPBERRY JAM

Makes about 3/4 cup (240 g)

Ingredients

1 cup (125 g) raspberries

2 tablespoons maple syrup

1 tablespoon cornstarch

Special Tools

Glass pint jar with lid

1. In a medium saucepan, combine the raspberries, syrup, and cornstarch and cook over medium-high heat. As you stir, the raspberries will break down and turn to liquid. Bring the mixture to a boil.

2. Reduce the heat to medium and cook and stir until the mixture coats the back of the spoon, 8 to 9 minutes.

3. Pour the mixture into the glass pint jar and let cool before sealing with the lid.

4. Store in the refrigerator for up to 4 weeks.

Brunch Board

A combination of breakfast and lunch—two of our three favorite meals of the day?! We're in! With bacon, eggs, pancakes, and fruit, this board rivals the hottest brunch spot in town.

Board Items

Scrambled eggs

Purina Beggin' Strips

Pup Pancakes (page 127)

Bacon Kale Cookies (page 128)

Raspberries

Blackberries

Pineapple chunks

Kiwi slices

Wiggles & Wags Bake Shop Brunchie Munchies

Supplies

Rectangular tray with sides

Oblong plate

Build Your Board

Center the oblong plate in the tray. Place the scrambled eggs, Beggin' Strips, and Pup Pancakes on the plate, each filling a third of the plate.

Add stacks of the Bacon Kale Cookies to the corners of the tray.

Fill in the bottom portion of the tray with the berries and the top portion with the pineapple and kiwi.

Separate the Brunchie Munchies waffle and toast shapes, then place the waffles along one side of the plate and the toast along the other side.

PUP PANCAKES

Makes 12 pancakes

Ingredients

1 large egg

1 tablespoon pure maple syrup

1 tablespoon sunflower oil, plus more for greasing

1 cup (240 ml) buttermilk

1 cup (125 g) whole wheat flour

1 teaspoon baking powder

1. In a medium bowl, whisk together the egg, syrup, oil, and buttermilk. In a small bowl, combine the flour and baking powder. Add the flour mixture to the egg mixture and mix just until combined. There may be some lumps in the batter.

2. Preheat a large skillet or griddle over medium heat for 3 to 4 minutes. Brush the skillet or griddle with a little oil. When hot, ladle small amounts of batter into the skillet or onto the griddle. When some bubbles have formed around the edges and the bottom is golden brown, flip the pancake. Continue to cook until the second side is golden brown. Repeat with the remaining batter.

3. Serve immediately. Store leftovers in an airtight container in the refrigerator for up to 2 days.

BACON KALE COOKIES

Makes 20 to 25 cookies

Ingredients

4 strips low-sodium bacon

1 cup (65 g) loosely packed, coarsely chopped kale

3 large eggs, divided

2 tablespoons coconut oil, melted

1 cup (125 g) whole wheat flour

¼ cup (30 g) all-purpose flour, for dipping

Special Tools

Cookie stamp or glass

1. Preheat the oven to 375°F (190°C; gas mark 5). Line a baking sheet with parchment paper or a silicone baking mat.

2. In a medium skillet, cook the bacon over medium-high heat until crisp, about 5 minutes per side. Transfer to a paper towel–lined plate to drain the fat. Let cool.

3. Add the bacon, kale, 2 eggs, coconut oil, and whole wheat flour to a food processor and process until the mixture is well combined and forms a soft dough.

4. Add the all-purpose flour to a small bowl. Form the dough into ¾-inch (2 cm) balls. Dip each dough ball into the flour so that only half of it is lightly covered in flour, then arrange the dough balls on the prepared baking sheet, flour sides up. Press the balls with the cookie stamp (or if you don't have one, use the bottom of a glass), flattening them to about ⅓ inch (8.5 mm) thick.

5. Beat the remaining egg in a separate small bowl. Brush the tops of the pressed cookies with the egg wash.

6. Bake until golden around the edges, 15 to 20 minutes. Let cool completely.

7. Store in an airtight container in the refrigerator for up to 5 days.

Playdate Board

Believe it or not, sometimes we get tired of playing with each other, which calls for a playdate! When we invite guests over, we want to make sure they not only have fun, but also enjoy delicious treats. Just try to keep the supervision to a minimum, because if your dog is anything like Olivia, privacy is demanded.

Board Items

Seedless watermelon

Cantaloupe

Milo's Kitchen Chicken Meatballs

Banana Balls (page 132)

Blueberries

Dingo Goof Balls

Supplies

3 Frisbees

Melon baller

Tennis balls

Build Your Board

Place the Frisbees upside down and slightly askew from one other.

Using the melon baller, make balls out of the watermelon and cantaloupe. Mix the fruit balls together on the top Frisbee.

Make a layer of Chicken Meatballs on the second Frisbee. Place the Banana Balls on top of the meatballs and layer blueberries on top.

Place the tennis balls on the bottom Frisbee and add the Dingo Goof Balls to the mix.

BANANA BALLS

Makes 14 balls

Ingredients

2 cups (180 g) rolled oats

2 tablespoons honey

4 tablespoons melted coconut oil, divided

1 medium ripe banana

½ cup (55 g) unsalted peanuts, finely chopped

1. Preheat the oven to 325°F (165°C; gas mark 3). Line a baking sheet with parchment paper or a silicone baking mat.

2. In a medium bowl, stir together the oats, honey, and 2 tablespoons of the coconut oil until well blended. Spread the oats on the prepared baking sheet.

3. Bake until golden, 12 to 15 minutes. Let cool.

4. Place about ½ cup (45 g) of the toasted oats in a shallow bowl for rolling. Set aside.

5. In a medium bowl, mash the banana. Stir in the remaining 2 tablespoons coconut oil. Add the the toasted oats not reserved for rolling and mix until incorporated and the mixture is well combined.

6. Scoop about 2 tablespoons of the mixture and form into a ball. Roll the ball in the oats and transfer to the prepared baking sheet. Repeat with the remaining mixture and toasted oats.

7. Refrigerate for 1 hour before serving or store in an airtight container in the refrigerator for up to 2 days.

Tail-gate Board

Unless it's the Puppy Bowl, we don't understand why the humans get so excited about a football game. That said, we never pass up an opportunity to spend time outside with Dad and his friends while enjoying this board with lots of tasty treats.

Board Items

Slider Buns (page 136)

True Chews Premium Grillers

Romaine lettuce

Baby carrots

Celery sticks

Three Dog Bakery Pet-zel Bites

Canine Carry Outs Hot Dog Minis

Pup Corn Plus Chicken & Cheddar Cheese

Great Choice Dog Puffed Treat

Supplies

Rectangular tray with sides

Build Your Board

Slice the Slider Buns, then build the sliders with the Premium Grillers and romaine lettuce. Place the sliders in the center of the tray.

Fill the corners of the tray with the carrots and celery sticks.

Fill the top of the tray with the Pet-zel Bites, the bottom with the Hot Dog Minis, the left side with the Pup Corn, and the right side with the Puffed Treats.

SLIDER BUNS

Makes 15 buns

Ingredients

1 large egg, separated

½ cup (115 g) unsweetened plain yogurt

½ cup (125 g) unsweetened applesauce

2 cups (250 g) whole wheat flour

1 teaspoon baking powder

1½ teaspoons sesame seeds

1. Preheat the oven to 350°F (175°C; gas mark 4). Line a baking sheet with parchment paper or a silicone baking mat.

2. In a small bowl, beat the egg white until foamy. Set aside.

3. In a medium bowl, combine the egg yolk, yogurt, and applesauce and mix until well combined. In another small bowl, stir together the flour and baking powder. Add the flour mixture to the yogurt mixture and mix until incorporated and a soft dough forms.

4. Scoop about 1½ tablespoons of dough and roll it into a ball. Place it on the prepared baking sheet and flatten with your palm to ½ inch (12 mm) thick. Repeat with the remaining dough.

5. Brush the tops with the beaten egg white and sprinkle with the sesame seeds.

6. Bake until the tops are domed and slightly cracked, 12 to 15 minutes. Let cool completely.

7. Store in an airtight container for up to 1 week.

Caturday Board

Because Theodore was such a trooper while we made this book, even helping us create some of the boards and assisting with the photo shoot, we wanted to include a board for our feline friends. Make this board on Caturday or any day of the week for your cat and you may have the next viral cat video.

Board Items

Catnip

Tuna Catnip Treats (page 140)

Rachael Ray Nutrish LoveBites

Rachael Ray Nutrish Wheelies

Feline Greenies

Temptations MixUps

Tiny Tiger Meaty Tenders Sticks

Supplies

Cat-shaped board

Small ramekin

Build Your Board

Fill the ramekin with catnip and place it in the center of the board.

Fill in the bottom of the board with the Tuna Catnip Treats and fill in the rest of the board with the store-bought treats.

Place 3 Meaty Tenders on each side of the ramekin on top of the treats to give your cat board whiskers.

TUNA CATNIP TREATS

Makes 50 treats

Ingredients

4 ounces (113 g) unsalted tuna, canned in water

1 egg

1 cup (125 g) whole wheat flour, plus more for dusting

1 tablespoon dried catnip

Special Tools

Mini fish-shaped cookie cutter

1. Preheat the oven to 350°F (175°C; gas mark 4). Line a baking sheet with parchment paper or a silicone baking mat. Drain and reserve the water from the can of tuna.

2. In a food processor, blend the tuna, egg, flour, and catnip until a dough forms. If the dough is too dry, add some of the reserved tuna water, a teaspoon at a time, until the dough holds together.

3. On a lightly floured surface, roll out the dough to ¼ inch (6 mm) thick. Use the cookie cutter to cut out the shapes and transfer them to the prepared baking sheet.

4. Bake until golden, 10 to 15 minutes. Let cool completely.

5. Store in an airtight container in the refrigerator for up to 1 week.

Milestone
BOARDS

Index

Recipe List

Resources

Boards

Anthropologie
www.anthropologie.com

KEPATO
www.amazon.com

Target
www.target.com

Supplies & Tools

Amazon
www.amazon.com

Ateco Baking Products
www.atecousa.com

Nordic Ware
www.nordicware.com

Williams Sonoma
www.williams-sonoma.com

Wilton
www.wilton.com

Treats

Chewy
www.chewy.com

PetSmart
www.petsmart.com

Molly's Barkery
www.target.com

Three Dog Bakery
www.threedog.com

Tractor Supply
www.tractorsupply.com

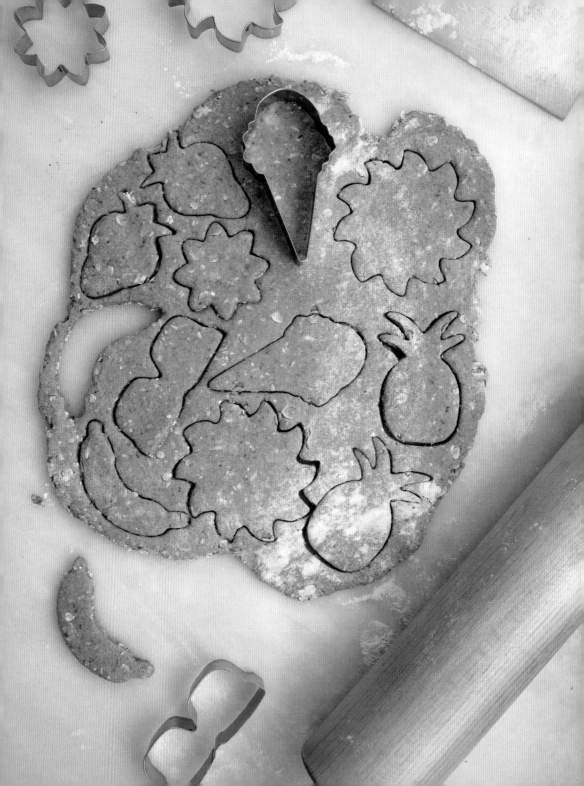

Graduation Day Board

Good dog! You did it! You graduated from obedience school, and now you will never get in trouble. Actually, that's not true. Case in point: Hammy. But in this moment, you can do no wrong, so have a little fun being a little bit disobedient by tearing into this board.

Board Items

Chicken Jerky (page 147)

Baby carrots

Celery sticks

Three Dog Bakery Soft Baked Peanut Butter & Banana Woofers

Merrick Power Bites

Three Dog Bakery Puppy Butters

Supplies

Long rectangular board

Build Your Board

Lay the Chicken Jerky across the center of the board.

Create a striped pattern by alternating the baby carrots and celery sticks on the top and bottom of the board.

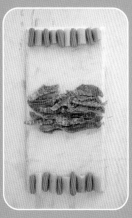

Working toward the center from the top and bottom of the board, add a row of Woofers, followed by a row of Power Bites, a row of Puppy Butters, and a second row of Power Bites closest to the Chicken Jerky.

CHICKEN JERKY

Makes about 25 pieces

Ingredients

2 boneless, skinless chicken breasts

2 teaspoons turmeric powder

Special Tools

Dehydrator (optional)

1. Preheat the oven or a dehydrator to 165°F (75°C). If using the oven, add a cooling rack on top of a sheet pan and set aside.

2. Cut the chicken into long, thin strips. Sprinkle the strips with the turmeric powder on both sides. Arrange the chicken strips on the prepared cooling rack or dehydrator sheets.

3. Dehydrate until dry and firm and yet still pliable, about 9 hours.

4. Wipe off any oil on the surface of the jerky and store it in an airtight container. No need to refrigerate.

Birthday Party Board

We're *always* referred to as Hammy AND Olivia, so our birthdays are the one day of the year we can be Hammy OR Olivia. And believe us, we maximize that twenty-four hours to the fullest and make sure we are spoiled to the hilt. We suggest you do the same for your pup with this festive board!

Board Items

Celebration Pupcorn (page 153)

Confetti Pupcakes (page 154)

Molly's Barkery Barkday Cupcakes Apple Cinnamon Flavor

Pork Chomps Assorted Crunchy Bones

Dog-safe sprinkles

Supplies

Rectangular board

Medium bowl

1 or 2 small cake pedestals

Pom-pom garland (optional)

2 small ramekins or pinch bowls

Build Your Board

Fill the medium bowl with the Celebration Pupcorn and place on the board.

Place the cake pedestals around the board. If using the pom-pom garland, lay it around the board and cake pedestals.

Arrange the Confetti Pupcakes on the pedestals and board. Fill in the open space on the board with the Molly's Barkery Cupcakes and the Crunchy Bones.

Fill the ramekins with sprinkles. Add more sprinkles to the table for a festive touch.

CELEBRATION PUPCORN

Makes 4 cups (240 g)

Ingredients

2 tablespoons sunflower oil, divided

2 tablespoons popcorn kernels

¼ package (2 ounces, or 60 g) cream cheese

1 tablespoon peanut butter

1 tablespoon honey

¼ cup (35 g) dog-safe sprinkles

1. Place a 2-foot (60 cm) sheet of parchment paper on the work surface.

2. Put 1 tablespoon of the oil in a large saucepan and place over medium heat. When hot, add a popcorn kernel and cover the pan with the lid. Once you hear the popcorn kernel pop, add the remaining kernels. Cover the pan and continually move it back and forth over the burner until the popping slows down to several seconds between pops. Remove the pan from the heat and spread the popcorn onto the prepared parchment paper to cool completely.

3. Meanwhile, add the cream cheese, peanut butter, and honey to a heatproof bowl. Microwave on high for 30 seconds. Whisk together. If the mixture is still firm, return to the microwave for 10-second intervals until the mixture is loose and can be drizzled.

4. Drizzle the peanut butter mixture evenly over the popcorn. Immediately top with the dog-safe sprinkles. Allow the toppings to set, about 1 hour.

5. Break apart the popcorn and serve or store in an airtight container for up to 1 week.

CONFETTI PUPCAKES

Makes 12 pupcakes

Ingredients

PUPCAKES

½ cup (120 g) vegan butter (not avocado), softened

½ cup (125 g) unsweetened applesauce

2 tablespoons honey

2 large eggs

⅓ cup (79 ml) sunflower oil

2 cups (280 g) gluten-free flour

2 teaspoons baking powder

¼ cup (35 g) dog-safe sprinkles, plus more for garnish (optional)

12 Chicken Biscuits (page 54) or store-bought mini bone-shaped biscuits, for garnish (optional)

FROSTING

1 package (8 ounces, or 227 g) cream cheese, softened

1 tablespoon cornstarch

1 tablespoon honey

Dog-safe food coloring (optional)

Special Tools

12-cup muffin pan

12 paper baking cups

Disposable piping bag with decorator tip (optional)

1. **To make the pupcakes:** Preheat the oven to 350°F (175°C; gas mark 4). Line the muffin pan with the paper baking cups.

2. In a medium bowl, combine the butter, applesauce, honey, eggs, and oil and mix until well combined. In a small bowl, stir together the flour and baking powder. Add the flour mixture to the butter mixture and mix just until combined. Stir in the dog-safe sprinkles. Fill each baking cup about three-quarters full with the batter.

3. Bake until lightly golden, 15 to 18 minutes. Let cool completely.

4. **Meanwhile, make the frosting:** In a medium bowl, combine the cream cheese, cornstarch, and honey and beat until fluffy, 2 to 3 minutes. Add food coloring, if using.

5. When the pupcakes are completely cool, spread the frosting on them with an offset knife or the back of a spoon, or, if desired, use a piping bag with a decorator tip to pipe the frosting onto the cakes. Garnish with more dog-safe sprinkles and a mini bone biscuit, if desired.

6. Store in an airtight container in the refrigerator for up to 5 days.

NOTE: For extra-tall frosting double the frosting recipe.

Gotcha Day Board

Gotcha day is like a second birthday! And though the focus of the day is on you, make sure to show your humans tons of love for adopting you and giving you an awesome home. And if you have a social media account, let everyone know the importance of adopting a pet.

Board Items

- Peanut Butter Coconut Bites (page 158)
- Redbarn Chew-A-Bulls Hydrant
- Curly kale leaves
- Foppers Pet Treat Bakery Birthday Peanut Butter Flavor Bone
- Strawberries
- Wiggles & Wags Bake Shop Coco-Moas Dog Cookie
- True Chews Chicken Bacon Recipe

Supplies

Rectangular board

Build Your Board

Place the Peanut Butter Coconut Bites in a mound on the center of the board.

Place a row of Hydrants along the top of board. Add a row of kale leaves below the Hydrants.

Center a Foppers Bone above the Peanut Butter Coconut Bites.

Surround the Peanut Butter Coconut Bites and the Foppers Bone with the strawberries.

Center the Coco-Moas on the bottom of the board, then flank them with the True Chews.

PEANUT BUTTER COCONUT BITES

Makes 12 bites

Ingredients

½ cup (45 g) unsweetened coconut flakes

½ cup (130 g) creamy peanut butter

1 tablespoon honey

¾ cup (70 g) oat flour

1. Line a baking sheet with parchment paper.

2. In a medium skillet, toast the coconut over medium heat, stirring constantly until golden brown. Transfer the toasted coconut to a shallow bowl and set aside.

3. In a medium bowl, combine the peanut butter, honey, and oat flour and mix until incorporated.

4. Scoop about 2 tablespoons of the mixture and form a ball. Roll the ball in the toasted coconut flakes to coat evenly, then place it on the prepared baking sheet. Repeat with the remaining mixture and toasted coconut.

5. Refrigerate for 1 hour before serving or store in an airtight container in the refrigerator for up to 1 week.

Bark Mitzvah Board

You can't skip out on tradition, not even for your dog. If your dog is Jewish, we've got the perfect board to celebrate their Bark Mitzvah—see what we did there?

Board Items

Three Dog Bakery Crunchy Beg-als

Doggie Rugelach (page 162)

Plain cream cheese

Honey

Dried apricots

Pear slices

Apple slices

Blueberries

Colby Jack cheese slices, cut into bite-size squares

Fresh figs

Blueberries

Three Dog Bakery Lick'n Crunch! Carob & Peanut Butter Sandwich Cookies

Three Dog Bakery Soft Baked Peanut Butter & Banana Woofers

Wiggles & Wags Bake Shop Short & Sweet

Supplies

Rectangular board

Small ramekin

Honey pot

Build Your Board

Create a river of Begals from the top-right corner of the board to the bottom-left corner.

Fill the other two corners with the Doggie Rugelach.

Fill the ramekin with the cream cheese and add honey to the honey pot. Place the ramekin on the top of the board and the honey pot on the bottom.

Fill in the space between the cream cheese ramekin and Rugelach with the dried apricots.

Lay the pear and apple slices along the left side of the Beg-al river.

Fill in the space between the Beg-al river and honey pot with the blueberries and cheese squares.

Fill in the remaining space with the figs, more apple slices, Sandwich Cookies, Woofers, and Short & Sweet cookie treats.

DOGGIE RUGELACH

Makes 12 rugelach

Ingredients

FILLING

¼ cup (25 g) unsalted peanuts

2 tablespoons dried cranberries

¼ cup (30 g) carob chips

DOUGH

1 cup (125 g) gluten-free flour, plus more for dusting

¾ package (6 ounces, or 170 g) cream cheese, softened

¼ cup (60 ml) buttermilk

1 large egg, beaten

Special Tools

Pizza cutter

1. Preheat the oven to 350°F (175°C; gas mark 4). Line a baking sheet with parchment paper or a silicone baking mat.

2. **To make the filling:** Place the peanuts, cranberries, and carob chips in a food processor and pulse until finely chopped. Set aside.

3. **To make the dough:** In a medium bowl, combine the flour, cream cheese, and buttermilk and mix until incorporated and the mixture forms a soft dough. Form the dough into a smooth ball and flatten it slightly.

4. On a lightly floured surface, roll out the dough into a 12-inch (30 cm) circle with a rolling pin. Scatter the filling evenly over the dough, all the way to the edges. Press down lightly on the filling so that it sticks to the dough.

5. Using a pizza cutter, cut the dough into 12 equal wedges. Starting from the wide side, roll up each wedge and place it, with the pointy end tucked under, on the prepared baking sheet. Repeat with the remaining wedges. Brush the tops with the beaten egg.

6. Bake until golden brown, 20 to 25 minutes. Let cool completely.

7. Store in an airtight container for up to 5 days.

About the Authors

These two might not have the longest legs or the fluffiest tails, but what they lack in canine stature, they make up for in personality. Olivia is an eight-year-old, tricolor corgi. She was born in Las Vegas and never had to leave because we're Vegas locals. She's 27 pounds (12.2 kg) of pure sass and takes great pride in ruling the house from her bed. She is very picky when it comes to the pillows she lies on, the furniture she sleeps on, and the food she eats. So, we joke that she's our resident diva. If they were to ever make a dog version of the movie *Clueless*, Olivia would certainly star as Cher Horowitz. She was an only child for two years before we brought Hammy into our lives.

Hammy is a six-year-old, red-and-white corgi who was born on the farms of North Carolina. When we first saw Hammy on a breeder's website, we immediately fell in love and knew that he was going to be the perfect addition to our furry family. He's a big sweetheart that loves giving kisses (especially if he knows there's a treat in your pocket). The only thing bigger than Hammy's heart is his appetite. He loves shadowing Chris in the kitchen, so he's now the appointed sous chef whenever we cook. These two furballs pack so much personality into their tiny frames, and their nine million social media followers love tuning in to their daily shenanigans. Our family's mission to spread daily smiles to millions around the world is led by this dynamic, doggy, brother-sister duo.